"Calming and soothing, bright and fun, Carol's poems capture the mature heart and the essence of living. The Poet's circle grew when Carol put pen to paper recently."
- Barbara Bloodgood, Therapeutic Yoga Instructor

"I especially love how Carol's words have the ability to bring healing to those that are blessed and fortunate enough to read them. They resonate long after the first reading."
- Sabrina Fritts, Associate Instructor for The Reconnection, Reconnective Kids! Facilitator

Bring Poetry to Life is a treasure! Reading a poem would be a delightful way to begin the day or close it. Carol has created a wonderful collection of poems that I will enjoy reading over and over and giving as gifts to those I love. Thank you Carol for sharing your talent with the world!"
- Lisa Shultz, Co-Creator of *Speaking Your Truth* and Owner and Founder of Women, Wine, and Wellness. www.LisaShultz.com

"Be sure to read *Bring Poetry To Life* with a box of tissues. The beautiful poetry of Carol Calkins will make you laugh, ponder and cry - all things that I need to do more of. I hope you put this book on the top of your reading list."
- Angel Tuccy, Best Selling Author of *Lists That Saved My Life* and *Lists That Saved My Business*

"Carol's poetry is a wonderful example of the beauty and wisdom that happens when a person follows her own energetic guidance and heart connected vision – creativity flows. These thoughtful and loving poems about life, love, family, death and birth are a sweet reminder of all of life's joys."
- Cathy and Gary Hawk, Partners of Clarity International® and co-authors of *Creating the Rest of Your Life*©, *An Atlas for Manifesting Success & Excellence in Life and Work*, and *Get Clarity*©, *Clarity of Energy, Vision, Focus and Action*

"The poems in *Bring Poetry to Life* consist of the most beautiful combination of synergistic language to inspire your life and touch your heart. Read one and you'll be begging for more."
— Andrea Costantine, Co-Author of *Speaking Your Truth* and *How to Bring Your Book to Life This Year*

"I appreciate the 'slice of life' approach that Carol Calkins uses to express the energy and emotions of everyday events. Her philosophy is simple, clean and easy to relate with. Ms. Calkins shares a love of life that inspires me to look at my life from a more grateful perspective."
- Ruth Sharon, M.S., LPC, RYT, Licensed Professional Counselor, Registered Yoga Teacher, Wellness Coach, www.energyforlife.us

"Your poetry touches my heart and soul! Your friendship blesses my life!"
- Cindy Cleveland, RScP, RN

"I have watched as Carol's amazing gift of poetry has come to the world in a fast-rushing river of creativity and love. How lucky we are to have her words capture our most special feelings and life's best moments. We all cannot wait to watch this love flow and touch the world. Congratulations Carol!"
- Betsy Wiersma, World Renown Motivational Speaker, Author, and Founder of CampExperience™

"Carol's poetry reminds us to treasure each heart-to-heart connection and the special moments they create. An inspiring observation of life, love and legacy!"
- Marie Kirkland, Spiritual Life Coach, Speaker and author of *Align Your Life*

"Bring Poetry to Life is an inspiration to recognizing life is the most beautiful poetry as we open our eyes to each moment."
- Marjorie Staum, Minister at Mile Hi Church
http://milehichurch.org/ministers/associate_ministers.asp

Bring *Poetry* to Life

Carol Calkins, PhD

Bring Poetry to Life
www.bringpoetrytolife.com
Copyright © 2010 Carol Calkins, PhD and Healing Heart, LLC

Cover Art: Madeleine O'Connell oil on canvas, copyright 2010 www.MWOConnell.com
Illustrations: Trish Bonati
Readers: Kerrie Bathje and Melissa Caron
Editing by Andrea Costantine
Layout/Design: Melissa Levad
Author Photograph by Kimberly Anderson Photography

Printed in the United States of America
First Edition
ISBN 978-1-453-85985-8

*Dedicated to my dear friend Linda Frawley who left us sooner
than we had hoped yet she touched and healed the hearts of so many.
Your passing inspired my poetry and made me realize the importance
of sharing my gifts with the world.*

*A special thanks to my wonderful husband Mike Calkins for his
unending love, devotion and support. You are my best friend,
confidante and love of my life.*

*With joyful gratitude to my daughter and son-in-law Katrina and Ray
Dorow who have truly been blessings in my life. They are giving me the
thrill of a lifetime by bringing my first grandchild into the world.*

Exotic Woman

Exotic Woman
Graced this place
Surrounded by plants and flowers
Observed her ways for many lovely hours

The lyrical voices of the birds
Sang sweetly of her exquisite beauty
A softness and subtle power
Her eyes mysterious and hypnotizing

Silky hair pulled back and full
Frames her face divinely
Smooth curves and regal angles
Wisdom and knowledge sublimely

When she speaks
All listen closely
Words flow from her sensuous lips
Amazing spirit with great intensity

Exotic Woman
Graced this place
Surrounded by plants and flowers
Observed her ways for many lovely hours

Inspired by cover art by Madeleine O'Connell

TABLE OF CONTENTS

Special People Special Moments

Endings

Introduction

In January 2010, a cool winter day in Colorado drifted slowly into a frigid night as the fated news was delivered to me. After a tiring battle with cancer my dear friend Linda was now at peace. While enduring this heartbreaking loss my energy and determination enabled me to rally around friends and family in celebration of Linda's everlasting memory. It was within the following days that the shining beauty of our treasured friendship became my passionate inspiration to bring words of healing, emotion and laughter to the world in the form of poetry.

I began to think and hear in poetry with words and phrases coming to me throughout the day. At first I would jot down words on anything I could find including sitting in a restaurant with my husband and writing on a cocktail napkin. Then I began carrying around a small spiral notebook that eventually evolved into a beautiful journal. As people would speak with me I would sense their emotions and find myself saying or thinking *sounds like a poem is coming on*. I found writing and sharing my poems became healing for me and for others. People started to ask me to write poems for them about a variety of situations they or others were experiencing in their lives. I began creating personal customized poems for those around me; and it became clear that this was my gift to share with the world.

The end of May 2010 I received what I thought was a Birthday card from my daughter and son-in-law in South Africa. Instead it was a card letting me know that I was going to be a Grandmother in January 2011. Talk about emotions. Excitement, elation, the thrill of the anticipated arrival was delightful and exhilarating. That brought on a wave of poems about growth of life, beginnings, and all that new life entails.

As I began to write more and more poetry, I realized I had at least one book to share with the world. That's when the title of this book *Bring Poetry to Life* came to me. This book is a glimpse of what shapes some of life's most powerful and poignant moments and includes three major sections Beginnings, Special People Special Moments, and Endings.

Now that my everyday experience is filled with poetry, I have two other books in the works. One focuses on life's challenges and searching for self and the other is a book of poetry for children that was inspired by my great nephew who is a poet extraordinaire at the age of 10 years old. I'm grateful to him and all my family and friends past and present who have inspired me and have enjoyed and been uplifted by the poetry I've shared with them thus far. I know now that bringing poetry to the world is my new found path, and it's thrilling to have discovered my gift and to share it with you and so many others. My hope is that you find peace and joy as you read *Bring Poetry to Life*.

Carol Calkins, PhD

Beginnings

What Happens in a Second

What Happens in a Second
Life begins and then it ends

What Happens in a Second
You come across a friend

What Happens in a Second
Marriage bond is complete

What Happens in a Second
A child is conceived

What Happens in a Second
Sun peeks above horizon

What Happens in a Second
Dusk sinks away to night

What Happens in a Second
A seed breaks ground to nature

What Happens in a Second
Eyes meet and love awakens

What Happens in a Second
Forgiveness is accepted

What Happens in a Second
Life feels like its perfected

What Happens in a Second
Life begins and then it ends

New Life

New Life
Anxious to learn and grow
Open to numerous possibilities
Experiences to observe and absorb

New being
Nurtured and loved by all
Joyful delight and sweet
Experiences to do and see

New child
Playful and activity bound
Explore small world around
Experiences to seek and be found

New spirit
Alert and aware to grasp
Search to take in and realize
Experiences to know at last

New Life
Anxious to learn and grow
Open to numerous possibilities
Experiences to observe and absorb

I Still Remember the Day You Were Born

I Still Remember the Day You Were Born
A beautiful spirit so loved and adorn
Changed my world from that day on
Blessing has graced me like a swan on a pond

You were so perfect in every way
Healthy and happy each lovely day
Excited about life and all new adventures
Anxious to experience to play and have fun

As you grew older you explored the world
Willing to help others sharing with boys and girls
Loved other cultures and how people are different
Understanding global matters a peaceful perspective

A joy to all whose lives you have touched
Your beauty and wisdom contribute so much
My hope is that throughout every amazing day
You fully comprehend the many gifts you gave

I Still Remember the Day You Were Born
A beautiful spirit so loved and adorn
Changed my world from that day on
Blessing has graced me like a swan on a pond

Growth of Life

Growth of Life nothing beyond compare
Simple in ways yet extraordinaire
Creating a being unlike any other
The joy and the thrill to be a mother

Some feelings are off, some morning ills
Some brightly glow full blossoming shows
A beauty so dear a bond so divine
As mother and child together intertwined

Months pass by anticipation expands
Nature's wonderful cycle taking place again
A movement inside a push from within
What a delightful connection and a lovely union

The day is upon us
Celebration at hand
Family surrounding
A new life begins

Growth of Life nothing beyond compare
Simple in ways yet extraordinaire
Creating a being unlike any other
The joy and the thrill to be a mother

Such Sweet Little Energy

A blessing that's heaven sent
Precious gift creates synergy
Such Sweet Little Energy
Coming into our lives

The moment we felt you
A special being so true
Vibrations that are divine
Knowing everything is fine

When tensions arise
Comes as no surprise
There is peace in the air
Your calmness soon appears

Joyful angel is now around
Love and happiness fully abounds
Together forever with our beautiful child
An amazing miracle into our world

A blessing that's heaven sent
Precious gift creates synergy
Such Sweet Little Energy
Coming into our lives

No Worries My Dearest

No Worries My Dearest
Have no fears
Release anxiety
No need for tears

Gift of life
Coming your way
Creation so joyful
Anticipate the day

All you desire
Deserve to receive
Flows into your world
Perfectly conceived

Be patient with yourself
Experience calmness and peace
No matter what you do
Dreams will come true

No Worries My Dearest
Have no fears
Release anxiety
No need for tears

Unexpected Surprise

Unexpected Surprise
That's changing our lives
Thought it couldn't happen anymore
A new life for us to adore

All future plans seemed routine
Two of us with family and friends
Everything seemed to be on track
Interesting twists and turns on our path

Funny how when you least expect
Tiny miracle becomes gigantic
A divine blessing came our way
Filled with joy and fun each day

So when you feel settled in
Think life can't give another thing
Expect new and exciting events to occur
It's amazing what wonders will appear

Unexpected Surprise
That's changing our lives
Thought it couldn't happen anymore
A new life for us to adore

My Little Sweet Pea

It came to me
My loving child
You will always be
My Little Sweet Pea

There's something about
A grandchild so dear
Fills the heart
With joy and cheer

Sense your being
So close at hand
Know connection
Special bond to share

Loving soul
Delightful and pure
Share with the world
Someone so dear

It came to me
My loving child
You will always be
My Little Sweet Pea

Hearts of Hands

Hearts of Hands
As life expands
Beauty conveyed
Each lovely day

From within
Intertwined as one
Soon to separate
And become two

Love expressed
Exquisite and true
Unconditional
Between me and you

Family bond
Sharing with pleasure
Divine and pure
Cherish the treasure

Hearts of Hands
As life expands
Beauty conveyed
Each lovely day

My Little African Baby

My Little African Baby
Special indeed
Born across the ocean
A beautiful sight to see

Citizen of the world
Two countries call home
Understanding many cultures
One with humanity never alone

A child so precious
A spirit of peace
Brings joy to others
A sense of great ease

Touches hearts of humans
Connects loving souls
Shares knowledge and wisdom
A gift to young and old

My Little African Baby
Special indeed
Born across the ocean
A beautiful sight to see

Darling Daughter

Darling Daughter
Mother to be
Precious child
Is on its way

Gift of life
Blessing is a miracle
So delightful
Love that's divine

Gentle spirit
Linked as one
Mother and child
Next generation to come

Bond that's greater
Than can be imagined
Power from above
Unconditional love

Darling Daughter
Mother to be
Precious child
Is on its way

There isn't a Mother

There isn't a Mother
In the entire world
Who hasn't worried
About her child unborn

A special bond
Developing over time
Filled with love and great fondness
Happiness so sublime

This precious life
Growing inside
Sweet and fine
Being who is divine

Thank each day
For this amazing chance
To love completely
And be loved right back

There isn't a Mother
In the entire world
Who hasn't worried
About her child unborn

New Baby

New Baby
On the way
Precious being
Here to stay

New mother
Filled with joy
Thrilled for child
Girl or boy

New father
Excitement grows
New child
Much to know

New family
Together at last
Create a future
Memorable past

New Baby
On the way
Precious being
Here to stay

A Glimpse of a Grandchild

A Glimpse of a Grandchild
A generation to come
An enchanting experience
I know it will come

A delightful beginning
A blessing indeed
The bright shiny face
Filled with anticipation and joy

I remember my own child
As if it had just happened
But the difference is astonishing
With the love and perspective

The legacy is planted
The seed will full bloom
I know it's upon me
To be grandparent soon

A Glimpse of a Grandchild
A generation to come
An enchanting experience
I know it will come

Got a Card

Got a Card the other day
Thought to celebrate my birthday
Open up to my surprise
Going to be a Grandma

Began to shout and jump for joy
Hugged my husband what a guy
Emotions flooding through our souls
Happiness our mood way up high

First baby for my darling kids
Excitement for parents to be
Grandparents thrilled and ecstatic
Anticipating child we'll soon see

Our little girl is fully grown
A mother and child together now
Love and caring beautiful
Family bonding and anew

Got a Card the other day
Thought to celebrate my Birthday
Open up to my surprise
Going to be a Grandma

I Spoke to My Grandchild

I Spoke to My Grandchild
Just the other day
Told me to tell you
Soon on the way

Wanted to thank you
For bringing into our lives
Is so content and happy
To be part of this world

Heard you were special
Very loving and caring
Give to many others
Always generously sharing

Feels extremely fortunate
To have parents like you
Blessed to be together
All dreams have come true

I Spoke to My Grandchild
Just the other day
Told me to tell you
Soon on the way

Image of a Grandchild

Image of a Grandchild
Unmistakable and mystifying
A scan shows tiny features
Distinct in every way

A gentle noble face
Uncertain of resemblance
A knowingness is clear
Peace and harmony appears

Anxious in meeting
This new precious being
Anticipate the arrival date
Can hardly bear to wait

Look into those lovely eyes
Hear the baby laugh and sigh
Touch those small fingers and toes
Kiss the sweet one on the nose

Image of a Grandchild
Unmistakable and mystifying
A scan shows tiny features
Distinct in every way

Welcome to the World

Welcome to the World
Loving and gentle soul
Been walking on clouds
Heavenly beings around

Now you are joining us
Adding your light to our lives
We are thankful to experience this
Culmination of our dreams and wishes

What a glorious happening
Filled with joy and delight
A new spirit on the earth
Amazing brilliance so bright

Experience what's in store for you
Affection and warm feelings
Family and friends all together
Greet you on your journey of a lifetime

Welcome to the World
Loving and gentle soul
Been walking on clouds
Heavenly beings around

My Child, My Son

My Child, My Son
What a blessing in life
Watching you grow
Watching you learn

My boy, my son
What a joy to be around
Watching you play
Watching you run

Young man, my son
What a thrill to see your skills
Watching your talents
Watching your precious gifts

A man, my son
What a pleasure to know you
Watching you as a leader
Watching you share with others

My grandchild, my grandson
What a blessing in life
Watching you grow
Watching you learn

Child's View

Sometimes difficult to see
What's going on around me
Can't figure out what or who
Looking from a Child's View

World seems really huge
Uncertain how to do
Easy things new to me
Learn to act and to be

From my perspective
Others are tall
Surrounded by giants
Feel so small

Little fearful and unsure
Gentle touch so sincere
Sense of calmness as I hear
Soothing words of love is clear

Sometimes difficult to see
What's going on around me
Can't figure out what or who
Looking from a Child's View

Children of Glory

Children of Glory, children of hope
When you look at the world, find your head in a swirl
Remember the children pave future's way
Share in and nurture their love filled days

Confusion and chaos may be the state of affairs
Political strife and economic disaster declared
The earth in a peril warming planet or green
Bringing forth to the nations a fear that is keen

When all else seems lost and everything failed
When sadness and poverty appears to prevail
Raise up your eyes and open your hearts
A new beginning is here to start

The perception of children delightful and new
Providing a perspective that is certainly true
A deep down desire to learn and to grow
Dreams for the taking and so much to know

So experience may bring wisdom
And education expand scope
But the real teachers of life
Are those who are most childlike

Children of Glory, children of hope
When you look at the world, find your head in a swirl
Remember the children pave future's way
Share in and nurture their love filled days

World Changer Light Up the World

What if we tell our children to live their dreams from the start
Experience each day with passion coming from the heart
Share your gifts with others, living life fulfilled
Be a World Changer Light Up the World

If we raised our children so they always knew
They could make a difference depending on what they do
Make a contribution to everyone they touch
Add value caring for the human race and helping so much

As they gain knowledge and wisdom
And a better understanding of what's to come
Their sense of self and achievement
Brings forth the power of accomplishment

As their hopes turn to reality
And each individual life improves
The transformation of this planet
Becomes joy, peace and harmony

What if we tell our children to live their dreams from the start
Experience each day with passion coming from the heart
Share your gifts with others, living life fulfilled
Be a World Changer Light Up the World

Through the Eyes of a Child

Through the Eyes of a Child
World looks bright and vivid
Not a big picture at all
Small details play in it

Through the eyes of a teen
World is so focused
Blinders to the full scope
See only what they know

Through the eyes of an adult
World grows bigger in size
Life brings on challenges and hope
More understanding realized

Through the eyes of a senior
World becomes calm and clear
Know that having perspective
Is what one must hold most dear

Through the Eyes of a Child
World looks bright and vivid
Not a big picture at all
Small details play in it

Enchanting Child

Enchanting Child
Makes me smile
Lovely voice to hear
Makes my heart sing

Sweetest little being
I've ever seen
Cherish the happiness
Watch joyful frolicking

Dancing all around
Notice sights and sounds
In the sky and on the ground
Beautiful world surrounds

Laughter can be heard
Such precious words
Excitement in the air
Enjoy life without a care

Enchanting Child
Makes me smile
Lovely voice to hear
Makes my heart sing

Special People
Special Moments

Mother and Daughter

Mother and Daughter together forever
No matter apart by distance or time
Hearts connected deeply within
Lives intertwined beautifully divine

Legacy passed down generation to generation
Family cohesion from strength and love
Traditions created and shared with relations
Extending joy and happiness to so many others

Mother and Daughter a special bond
Unlike any union seen around the world
Sharing life's challenges and amazing wonders
Knowing each other's feelings, thoughts and dreams

At times conflicts and tensions do arise
No possible way to attempt to disguise
Meaningful affection and caring declared
Between these lovely bright spirits eternally

Mother and Daughter together forever
No matter apart by distance or time
Hearts connected deeply within
Lives intertwined beautifully divine

My Mom

An extraordinary woman once walked this earth
Bringing laughter and joy and so much mirth
Everyone she met felt a sense of being home
So blessed to say this lovely spirit is My Mom

She had a special way of lifting you up
No matter how difficult life's challenges appeared
She'd bring clear perspective to every circumstance
Once encountering her you just wanted to dance

Sometimes it's hard to believe this amazing person ever lived
No one could be this wonderful and so willing to give
She had a unique gift that is rarely seen in time
I knew I could just call her and everything would be fine

It's been more than 20 years since she passed this way
I think of her beauty and love nearly every day
What she shared with me and so many others
Hope for a glorious life and to be the very best mother

An extraordinary woman once walked this earth
Bringing laughter and joy and so much mirth
Everyone she met felt a sense of being home
So blessed to say this lovely spirit is My Mom

Thoughts of a Special Woman

Thoughts of a Special Woman
Come to mind time to time
An extraordinary person
Blessed to have her in my life

Spend precious moments
Sharing ourselves
Talks on every subject
Fun and games galore

Sometimes changes happen
Keeps us apart
Brought back together
Forever from the start

An exceptional being
Touches my heart eternally
With unconditional love
Soul sister from above

Thoughts of a Special Woman
Come to mind time to time
An extraordinary person
Blessed to have her in my life

My Father was an Amazing Man

My Father was an Amazing Man
First in his family to graduate college
Went on to become a pediatrician
Helping others by sharing his love and his knowledge

His medical calling was so much more
He improved life's conditions for countless young families
His dedication was to children and their numerous needs
He'd care for their spirits and heal what ails them

My dad had a passion that lasted a lifetime
A love for my mother, a bond pure and deep
Those around knew what they shared was unique
Their love permeated to family, friends and others they'd meet

He loved us four kids beyond comprehension
Knew we could do and be whatever we wanted
Lifted us up to strive for high standards
Helped us to be the best we could be

My dad was a true friend to those in his life
He stood by them when they were in strife
Regardless of the problem or difficulty at hand
He was there as a supportive and compassionate man

My Father was an Amazing Man
First in his family to graduate college
Went on to become a pediatrician
Helping others by sharing his love and his knowledge

Our Father

Our Father had a challenging life
Filled with many highs and lows
And yet he was a loving man
To everyone he greets and knows

Lost his wife way too soon
Brood too young, not on their own
Did his best to meet their needs
Not always easy to succeed

Firm but caring to his kids
Gave them guidance when he could
As adults didn't interfere
Let them live as they would

A man special in all he did
Kindness and wisdom in how he lived
A quiet life, model for all
Amazing and true in what he'd give

Our Father had a challenging life
Filled with many highs and lows
And yet he was a loving man
To everyone he greets and knows

Parents

Parents give so much
To their children as they grow
With support and guidance
They learn until they know

Lessons of life
Meaning and understanding
Letting them go
To do for themselves

Somewhere in life
A transition takes place
The role of the parent
Shifts unexpectedly about

The child whose grown
Becomes the caregiver now
Helping their parents
Live a more comfortable life

Parents give so much
To their children as they grow
With support and guidance
They learn until they know

Love at First Sight

Once in a million
Or less often than that
Two people's eyes meet
And it's Love at First Sight

A match made in heaven
So distinctive and pure
They know instantly
And are absolutely sure

They were meant for each other
Always were and always will be
Can tell by their deep connection
And everyone else can also see

Splendid love through and through
Affection and fondness so true
Soulmates forever more
Special marriage that's adorn

Once in a million
Or less often than that
Two people's eyes meet
And it's Love at First Sight

Our First Kiss

Our First Kiss, a gentle kiss
With softness to the touch
A lovely sense of energy
Creating light between us

At that wonderful instant
Time and space stood still
And surrounded us with
A brilliant sphere radiant and true

Eyes transfixed, our beings joined
New and fresh feelings upon us
Anticipation of what's yet to come
Awareness of delight and joy

For that moment, that special moment
Both sensed a new beginning
Giving hope for the future
A beautiful future with endless possibility

Our First Kiss, a gentle kiss
With softness to the touch
A lovely sense of energy
Creating light between us

Lovers Laughter

Lovers Laughter
Joyously frolic together
Intimate moments for everything
Two hearts connect and happily sing

Best friends forever
Share special times galore
Fondness, inspiration and so much more
Glorious bond no condition can sever

Companions in all things
Play and travel on wings
Explore and adventure far and wide
Always by each other's side

Soulmates from the start
Whether together or apart
A love and caring so strong
Existing as one eternally long

Lovers Laughter
Joyously frolic together
Intimate moments for everything
Two hearts connect and happily ever after

Love is a Blessing

Love is a Blessing
Created on high
Gives a warm feeling
Brings on a sweet sigh

Starts with a spark
Cozy stroll in the park
Hold hands on a walk
Chat, giggle and talk

Hugs of affection
Kisses of passion
Fondness grows stronger
Emotions last longer

Deep connection unfolds
Brings joy on so bold
Opens up hearts
Divine from the start

Love is a Blessing
Created on high
Gives a warm feeling
Brings on a sweet sigh

Marriage a New Beginning

Marriage a New Beginning
Filled with joy, happiness and love
A bond divinely created
Watched over from up above

Brings two hearts together
Separate in some ways yet one
Words of commitment spoken
Vows of devotion quietly shared

Family and friends surround you
Radiating affection all around
Vitalizing your new lives together
Enlivening deep love you have to give

For marriage has such treasures
Providing life's greatest pleasures
Feel the fondness and affection
Now that your lives truly intertwine

Marriage a New Beginning
Filled with joy, happiness and love
A bond divinely created
Watched over from up above

Love of My Life

Love of My life
What a delight in my world
We are fortunate indeed
Following our path wherever it leads

Understanding and compassion
Joy and good cheer
Adventurous travels
Having fun everywhere

A joining so perfect
Connection is strong
Linking our spirits
Mind, body and soul

A gift we've been given
Precious and pure
Blessings surround us
Happiness appears

Love of My life
What a delight in my world
We are fortunate indeed
Following our path wherever it leads

Marriage a Gift of Love

Marriage a Gift of Love
Blessings from up above
Connecting two sacred souls
Together uniquely as one

A bond that has been found
Whether talking or without a sound
Something special is there for sure
Holding hands with someone so dear

With all our loved ones around
Shared vows of love and praise
How wonderful as cheers abound
Amazing celebration of the day

Our lives are joined completely
A precious time so sweetly
Such joy and moments of glory
Forever as part of our story

Marriage a Gift of Love
Blessings from up above
Connecting two sacred souls
Together uniquely as one

As Each Day Passes

As Each Day Passes
I can't recall
A moment in time
Not filled with awe

Life together
Has been a delight
Creating memories
Morning and night

We found a love
So deep and true
A bond that's perfect
Between me and you

Whether home or traveling
To faraway places
Our experience together
Is one of amazement

As Each Day Passes
I can't recall
A moment in time
Not filled with awe

My Forever Love

I came across a glorious moment
A gift was given to me by life
A special time to always cherish
My first encounter with My Forever Love

We walked and talked for hours
Sharing details of our hearts and dreams
We played and laughed together
And time stood still eternally

Day turned to evening and then to night
Stars were twinkling in the sky
The moon was full so very bright
Our faces glowed with such delight

From that beginning our lives did bond
Devoted to each other affection abound
Traveled the world with adventure around
Created our home with beauty and peace

Years have passed filled with so much joy
Challenges face us success in each one
My confidante, best friend, companion in all
What a blessing to be loved unconditionally

I came across a glorious moment
A gift was given to me by life
A special time to always cherish
Lifelong encounters with My Forever Love

Marriage a Spiritual Bond

Marriage a Spiritual Bond
Divinely conceived
Two hearts link as one
Perfection achieved

A match made in heaven
Brought together to share
Love, joy and affection
Make a glorious pair

Surrounded by loved ones
Supporting this bond
Value sacred vows
Connection profound

Beautiful joining
Delightful and pure
Union exciting
True love is here

Marriage a Spiritual Bond
Divinely conceived
Two hearts link as one
Perfection achieved

Sitting by My Honey

Sitting by My Honey
Enjoying the time
Such a wonderful feeling
Peaceful and sublime

When your sweetheart
Is your best friend
Confidante and companion
Happily together exploring hand in hand

Life is beautiful
Thrilling and exciting
Learning new things
The future is inviting

Delightful pleasures
Loving and divine
Feel the oneness
Raise our spirits high

Sitting by My Honey
Enjoying the time
Such a wonderful feeling
Peaceful and sublime

I Love You My Sweet One

I Love You My Sweet One
Amazing you are
Look up at the heavens
I see you my star

As wonder surrounds me
Wrapped close in your arms
Our hearts beat together
Our souls deeply bond

Blessed to be with you
Each day of my life
Relationship meaningful
As husband and wife

As years pass by
And decades too
The love we share
Runs pure and true

I Love You My Sweet One
Amazing you are
Look up at the heavens
I see you my star

Our Family Tree

Our Family Tree
Know a few generations
Life's amazing creation
World that was meant to be

Roots go deep
History to keep
Spreads all around
A solid foundation

Trunk is our world
Family and friends surround
Experience is solid and strong
Legacy grows and lasts so long

Branches spread out
All directions no doubt
Produce the next generation
As ancestral spirit moves on

Our Family Tree
Know a few generations
Life's amazing creation
World that was meant to be

Family Reunion

A time to come together with family members
Who you sometimes speak with but are rarely seen
Catch up on happenings and lots of news
A Family Reunion will be fun and amuse

Hope it happens for all the right reasons
Join loved ones during various holiday seasons
Celebrations of all sorts with joy and elation
Birthdays, weddings and graduations

Too often only see each other when there's been a loss
Sad but true at such a terrible cost
Tears and emotions flow in all we say
Sorrow is the primary theme of the day

Don't wait too long to bring everyone around
Take some action so happiness will be found
Connect today getting updates and more
Special ones sharing lovely moments you fully adore

A time to come together with family members
Who you sometimes speak with but are rarely seen
Catch up on happenings and lots of news
A Family Reunion will be fun and amuse

Family

Don't lose touch with Family
Too important to the essence of life
See loved ones as often as you can
Their special connection is profound

It brings forth collective history
Common characteristics and ancestry
Lively stories from the past
Shared with others will always last

Family ties can be deeper than most
Simultaneously make a toast
To the ones who came before
Those not with us anymore

Raise your spirits high
Look around and with a sigh
Praise the experiences you've had together
Know there exists a bond that lasts forever

Don't lose touch with Family
Too important to the essence of life
See loved ones as often as you can
Their special connection is profound

Family of Friends

Family of Friends
Bonds unlike no others
Connections made instantly
Unions lasting forever

Birthright is not necessary
Common folks not the judge
Living together not required
Nor gaps of time between us

For whenever we're together
Face to face or just talking
All distance in time or space
Disappears and our link regained

How blessed we truly are
To have this amazing connection
Our relationship so meaningful
Both profound and softly gentle

Family of Friends
Bonds unlike no others
Connections made instantly
Unions lasting forever

Focus on Family

Focus on Family
Brings about good cheer
Support from your loved ones
Nothing can compare

Not always easy
Life can seem crazy
Speed of the world
Puts mind in a whirl

Distractions all around
Keeps other things in view
Need to change perspective
See importance of relations

Realize the fullness
Close around you all the time
Precious beings in your life
Create love, joy and happiness

Focus on Family
Brings about good cheer
Support from your loved ones
Nothing can compare

A Lovely Life This Is

A Lovely Life This Is
Enjoy each moment fully lived
A sense of power deep within
Know how to act and clearly win

Happy to be filled with laughter and joy
Feel in my heart a spirit sublime
Thoughts and perceptions magnificent
Know that all this is heaven sent

Times that seem out of sorts
Refocus and breathe a sigh of relief
Calmly walk forward without a care
Nothing like it can really compare

Brings forth happiness and delight
Amazing beauty all in sight
Uplifting and graciously at ease
Fills the world with total peace

A Lovely Life This Is
Enjoy each moment fully lived
A sense of power deep within
Know how to act and clearly win

Value of Friendship

Value of Friendship
Few experiences compare
Close loving connection
True lifetime bond is rare

Come upon a relationship
Where you are totally yourself
Hold it close to your heart
Lest it may come apart

Share all your successes
Expose flaws and confessions
Be vulnerable as a child
Loved deeply all the while

Amazing times together
Whether playful or deep
Know something is special
Lifelong sharing to keep

Value of Friendship
Few experiences compare
Close loving connection
True lifetime bond is rare

My Sisters are Special in My Life

My Sisters are Special in My Life
Somewhat different but a lot alike
Been there for me when I'm in need
Supportive of all my desires and my dreams

My sisters are my closest friends
Will be there for me to the end
Whether during times of sadness and tears
Or happiness and joy through the years

Have such fun memories of growing up
Especially when we'd giggle and laugh
Or just get mad and draw battle lines
Whatever the case it would always end fine

Nearly six decades been there for me
Gratitude as we still play and can just be
Together and connecting so frequently
Extraordinary women best friends indefinitely

My Sisters are Special in My Life
Somewhat different but a lot alike
Been there for me when I'm in need
Supportive of all my desires and my dreams

Mother Dear

Mother Dear
Always seem to compare
Want to be like you
Caring, loving and true

When things were rough
You'd gently listen
Hear my concerns
Help me learn

In happy times
We'd dance and laugh
Spin and swirl
Express joy in our world

Daughter now mother to be
Hopes baby loves her as she loves me
No doubt special bond exists
Mother-child love forever persists

Mother Dear
Always seem to compare
Want to be like you
Caring, loving and true

Saying I Love You

Saying I Love You
Is not always easy
To convey deep emotions
With sincerity and devotion

A gift so exquisite
Receive as it's given
Heart to heart connection
Brings a fullness to living

Be aware of how spoken
Must come from deep within
Repeating with a casual tone
May leave an empty feeling

Words more powerful
Than any found around
Share them from a place of joy
True happiness will abound

Saying I Love You
Is not always easy
To convey deep emotions
With sincerity and devotion

Women My Forever Sisters

Women My Forever Sisters
Filled with beauty and charm
Holding a hand out to me
Extending supportive arms

No matter what life brings my way
Whether turbulent or tender
I always know my sisters are there for me
Sharing all of life's amazing journeys

My sisters are the ones in life
Who help me to be my authentic self
To laugh and play and shed a tear
Living each moment with full pleasure

I look around my travels each and every day
With wide open eyes I know to surely see
Many women who are and may be
A true and beautiful loving sister to me

Women My Forever Sisters
Filled with beauty and charm
Holding a hand out to me
Extending supportive arms

Lovely Lady

Lovely Lady
Beauty so deep
Let cares fade away
Let your soul be at peace

Lovely Lady
Eyes glimmer so bright
Dance each night away
With such stunning grace

Lovely Lady
Give fully from the heart
Share your life with others
Let your love shine about

Lovely Lady
Receive life's gifts
Open to possibilities
With joy and confidence

Lovely Lady
Beauty so deep
Let cares fade away
Let your soul be at peace

Women of Power

Women of Power
Women of strength
Success in all things
To the greatest extent

Absorbing much wisdom
Gathering the view
Extending a hand
Helping those in need too

Knowing your gifts
Sharing them with others
Clear on your vision
Of what life can bring

Being of service
To so many people
Giving love and guidance
Throughout the world

Women of Power
Women of strength
Success in all things
To the greatest extent

Young Women Yet to Come

My hope is to fully share
With Young Women Yet to Come
Life's lessons learned and wisdom obtained
Guiding their life's journey along the way

As each struggle comes up
And they look for luck
To handle issues that do arise
Look within for answers deep inside

Time speeds quickly by
As they grow and mature
Focusing energy on personal dreams
Strengthening aspects of self-esteem

Both sadness and celebrations do arrive
As milestones of life move on by
As future teachers for countless others
Be true to yourself in all that you do

My hope is to fully share
With Young Women Yet to Come
Life's lessons learned and wisdom obtained
Guiding their life's journey along the way

Best Friends

Sometimes there is someone you meet
May or may not happen instantly
Fulfills your wants and your needs
Become Best Friends to the end

Not from a place of selfishness
Generous and kind, nothing less
Holds you deep in their heart
A special connection seems to start

Sense of a closeness that's here for life
Through happiness and situations of strife
Brings support and joy in every way
Have fun together and love to play

A precious being, special to many
Shares delight and precious gifts aplenty
Scope of impact is truly awesome
Spreads wide and vast like the oceans

Sometimes there is someone you meet
May or may not happen instantly
Inspires your hopes and your dreams
Best Friends forever in all it seems

Life is a Joy

Life is a Joy
Live, love and laugh
Spend time with special ones
Share and have fun

Know it is priceless
Moments together
Exceptional occasions
In your heart forever

Gather up family and friends
Fill days and nights with bliss
Realize the amazing value
Thrill not meant to miss

Experience play and leisure
Feel wonders and pleasure
Frolic and prance around
Revealing hilarious sounds

Life is a Joy
Live, love and laugh
Spend time with special ones
Share and have fun

They Travel the World

They Travel the World
Bring love, joy and cheer
My daughter and son-in-law
Such gifts as they care

Adventures galore in many exotic places
Exciting activities experience loads of fun
Meet new people at their daily paces
Learn common practices and cultural ways

Make contributions to all they meet
Help women and children existing in need
To enhance their lives and their community
By serving others and giving unselfishly

Create friendships wherever they go
Spread understanding and encourage hope
Know true meaning to help others help themselves
Share special feelings that they have gently held

They Travel the World
Bring love, joy and cheer
My daughter and son-in-law
Such gifts as they care

Sometimes You Live a Lifetime

Sometimes You Live a Lifetime
Doing the best for sure
Knowing others don't perceive
Meaning of all your years

Shared a life with a special love
Who since has passed away
Children have grown and grandchildren too
Legacy of a full life completely renewed

Thinking back and pondering all
Seeing true value as I recall
Conflict at times never quite resolved
Maybe with perspective finally it will dissolve

For we each see life with such different eyes
What is love to one may seem to another contrived
My hope for the future and what's yet to come
That understanding will be found within each loving one

Sometimes You Live a Lifetime
Doing the best for sure
Knowing others don't perceive
Meaning of all your years

Remember Life is Precious

Remember Life is Precious
Can change in an instant
Don't take for granted
Left wondering why and what if

With a blink of an eye
Things become different
A twist of fate
Just can't prevent

One day all seems fine
The next it's not
Have hope for the future
This too will pass by

Value time with loved ones
Enjoy being together
Share special moments
Bring pleasure and joy

Remember Life is Precious
Can change in an instant
Don't take for granted
Left wondering why and what if

A Light Hearted Soul

Have you ever met a Light Hearted Soul
During your journey on the earth
With a brilliant smile contagious with glee
Permeates throughout it's all we can see

It's a surprising thing to experience such grace
For these beings are of the brightest light
Whether confusion or chaos or in darkest hours
These beautiful spirits are full of aliveness

They radiate a beam, a powerful beam
Filled with joy, love and peace unyielding
When they're around there's often no sound
Except the glimmer of essence and beat of one's heart

These precious souls seem to possess such wisdom
In their simple and lovely ways
It is certainly clear that as they walk the world
We have been blessed by their delightful presence

Have you ever met a Light Hearted Soul
During your journey on the earth
With a brilliant smile contagious with glee
Permeates throughout it's all we can see

There are People Amongst Us

There are People Amongst Us who are special in many ways
Others may not see them as they walk through their life and days
These people may touch your life in a moment or weeks or years
And if you are a fortunate one, they give a glimpse of joy and cheer

They move quietly amongst us with little flair or fanfare
They are not special due to fame or fortune
Nor are they celebrities or heads of state
They are lovely, kind and giving souls who care
for others in an unpretentious way

As the months go by and we blink an eye,
it is so easy to miss this subtle beauty
For these special people bring comfort and
enduring love to those who pass their way
Somehow they sense our pain, understand our wants,
and with a gentleness give exactly what is needed

If truly lucky your paths may cross and you will be changed forever
Be thankful for every moment of every day for the happiness they bring
You have received a gift not given to all and blessings beyond your dreams

Pay attention and be alert, don't hesitate for a second
Keep your mind at peace and your heart wide open for
There goes another one along the way

There are People Amongst Us who are special in many ways
Others may not see them as they walk through their life and days
These people may touch your life in a moment or weeks or years
And if you are a fortunate one, they give a glimpse of joy and cheer

Ordinary People

Ordinary People
Cross life's path along the way
Listen very closely
What they share and what they say

Wisdom brings lessons
Conveys as valuable messages
In words, acts, and deeds
Helps others to succeed

Sometimes things do occur
Heroic by most measures
Humble feelings by that special one
Exceptional feats accomplished and done

Routine people pass by you see
Encountered most everyday
Transform and change as you perceive
Amazing beings here to stay

Extraordinary People
Cross life's path along the way
Listen very closely
What they share and what they say

Decade Changers

When we were young and eager
We'd set our sights to be
Enjoying visions of future perceived
Decade Changers our hopeful life to see

It seemed older folks had it made
Doing whatever they pleased every day
As we develop in time what does appear
Each stage brings different delightful years

Thirties and Forties were growing times
Families and friends playing so sublime
Activities galore and fun with the kids
We'd stay up late and really live

As fifties arrived became more introspective
Changing perspective being half a century old
Now in my sixties understanding overflows
My purpose is clear and my gifts so much more

When we were young and eager
We'd set our sights to be
Enjoying visions of future perceived
Decade Changers our hopeful life to see

Birthday Wish

Sending you a Birthday Wish
If together you'd get a hug and a kiss
Although experience this event far away
My love and best wishes are with you today

Birthdays are such precious and special days
Milestones of life with changes on the way
Know not what the future may bring
Celebration of joy as we gather and sing

Excitement of this glorious day
Anticipated like children having fun at play
To be with those who love us most
As they raise their glasses and make a toast

Whether young or old or in between
This day makes us feel like a king or a queen
Filled with current delight and high spirits too
Creating wonderful memories for a lifetime view

Sending you a Birthday Wish
If together you'd get a hug and a kiss
Although experience this event far away
My love and best wishes are with you today

Friends for Decades

Friends for Decades
Born within weeks
Celebrate each year
Happy Birthday cheer

Our children were youngsters
When we first met
So much has happened
Memories we'll never forget

Now they're grown up
Travel the world
Such wonderful people
We're fortunate indeed

As we sit together
Enjoy our annual lunch
Know the fondest of feelings
We share and cherish so much

Friends for Decades
Born within weeks
Celebrate each year
Happy Birthday cheer

Graduation

Graduation a momentous event
Years of study and much hard work
Be proud of all you've achieved and done
Accomplishing distinguished and lofty goals

Began this journey a bit overwhelmed
Focused on each class one at a time
Giving it your all and much, much more
One by one you completed with success

You deserve praise from those who care
Receiving many fantastic accolades
What you've completed is no easy feat
It's time to celebrate your studious deeds

In cap and gown you walk the stage
The audience applauds the gains you've made
A joy to partake of this memorable occasion
You deserve all the best the future can bring

Graduation a momentous event
Years of study and much hard work
Be proud of all you've achieved and done
Accomplishing distinguished and lofty goals

Graduation and College Bound

Have finally done it
Achieved my goals
Cheers for accomplishments
Graduation and College Bound

Adventure begins
As I open my eyes
A world so expansive
Hope to learn and be wise

Fun's in the picture
New friends and much more
Know I will enjoy it all
Journey as my future calls

Change will be significant
More decisions on my own
Rely on good judgment
I've fully internalized

Have finally done it
Achieved my goals
Cheers for accomplishments
Graduation and College Bound

Anniversary

Anniversary a joyous occasion
Filled with precious memories
Anticipating what's yet to come
Celebration of life's perfect bond

Our love has grown since we first met
We've shared many great experiences
Milestones and special events galore
Have brought us closer together even more

Quiet times have been exceptional too
Relaxing and just being me and you
A gentle connection yet quite strong
Knowing life together will last so long

Family is part of this extraordinary union
Relationships grow better with passage of time
Sharing tender moments and emotions so fine
Loving you dearly and knowing you'll always be mine

Anniversary a joyous occasion
Filled with precious memories
Anticipating what's yet to come
Celebration of life's perfect bond

The Holiday Season

The Holiday Season
What a glorious reason
Gather family and friends together
Regardless of the weather

Excitement and energy in the air
Joyful anticipation everywhere
A time to renew connections
Experience life's perfections

Important to realize
True value of this time
Stories of the past are shared
Deep feelings reappear

How fortunate to be
With ones we love so dear
Living the fullness of each day
Know the memories are here to stay

The Holiday Season
What a glorious reason
Gather family and friends together
Regardless of the weather

Holiday Season

Holiday Season so beautiful
Good cheer all around
Why do we search and struggle
For the perfect presents to be found

The true gifts are everywhere
Soon you'll see, feel, and hear
Open your eyes, mind, and heart
Warmth and love will appear

Melodious carols
Being sung with great joy
Uplifting each one of us
Like children and toys

Friendships renewed and made stronger
Reunions and parties galore
Appreciate that happiness and caring
Is what this festive time is really sharing

Holiday Season so beautiful
Good cheer all around
Why do we search and struggle
For the perfect presents to be found

Endings

If You Knew the Day You Die

If You Knew the Day You Die, would you live your life differently?

Would you look at those you love and convey
in your eyes and gestures your deep fondness?

Would you say the words you want to say and
speak them from a place of love and truth?

Would you do the things you love the most
that fill your heart and soul with joy?

Would you see the places you want to see,
but things always seemed to hold you back?

Would you look at the little things that pass you by
and notice the wonder and beauty around you?

Would you laugh more, play more, have more fun and frolic around?

Would you enjoy time together with those
you care about both in activity and silence?

Would you create more things of beauty and
fun and share those gifts with others?

Would you play in nature or elsewhere and
be thrilled by the joy of it all?

If You Knew the Day You Die, would you live your life differently?

Wake Up and Live

Why does it take the loss of a friend
For us to Wake Up and Live
When we hold in our hearts a beautiful gift
Why do we not fully cherish it

Friendship is such a valuable thing
Filled with joy, love, and happiness
Although we don't want to take it for granted
Maybe we just live too distracted

So next time you are with a precious friend
And the outside world is spinning around you
Take a moment and look into the eyes
Of someone there for you always

Embrace the time and space dearly
That surrounds you and your special friend
Realizing the significance of what you hold near
Nothing less than excellence a blessing so clear

Words like appreciation and gratitude are only words
You must share the feelings and express the fondness
For the bond you hold is an eternal bond
Bringing together love and gladness forever

Why does it take the loss of a friend
For us to Wake Up and Live
When we hold in our hearts a beautiful gift
Why do we not fully cherish it

There is No Time or Place

There is No Time or Place for a final farewell
You are forever in my thoughts
As life goes by rest assured
You are always within my heart

As the days turn to months
And months turn to years
There are many precious moments
Reminding me of you

These instants are mostly small
Just gentle nudges as they pass
And when they happen I hear your call
A magical bond together once again

Although they come and then they go
It brings forth beautiful feelings of you
It could be in a word or quiet sound
It is clearly reminiscent of you being around

I know your absence will be most profound
During times of celebration
A wedding day, a grandchild's birth
Life's milestones filled with love and joy

There is No Time or Place for a final farewell
You are forever in my thoughts
As life goes by rest assured
You are always within my heart

Racing to Reach the Finish Line

A wise man once said to me in his final days
For years I sensed much love and joy
I wonder why I spent my precious time
Racing to Reach the Finish Line

Wonderful children and a glorious wife
Experiencing each day full of life
Caring for others to help them heal
Existence so beautiful exuding appeal

Spent much time running hither and yon
Frantic at times, definitely out of control
I prided myself with my focused determination
My motto being "live life to the fullest"

I rushed to my work, I rushed again home
I rushed as I traveled to exotic lands and beyond
There was never a moment, A moment in time
Where pressure to live life with abandon
Didn't cross my mind

The lesson was a good one though little too late
Now I know the best practice is to stop and await
To appreciate life's gifts you must feel peace and wonder
Enriches the days by loving yourself as
You do so many others

A wise man once said to me in his final days
For years I sensed much love and joy
I wonder why I spent my precious time
Racing to Reach the Finish Line

Celebrate Life's Little Triumphs

No matter what life brings your way
No matter how tough things seem to be
Raise up your eyes to see what's true
Cherish and Celebrate Life's Little Triumphs

When facing challenges big or small
Not knowing quite what to believe or do
Your command of your thoughts are powerful
Cherish and Celebrate Life's Little Triumphs

When the pain of existence is too much to bear
And words of encouragement are hard to hear
When life seems too difficult to even go on
Cherish and Celebrate Life's Little Triumphs

When the loss of a dear one is nearly upon you
And you feel your grasp of reality slipping away
Thoughts of no longer being hurt so deeply
Do your best to Celebrate Life's Little Triumphs

Give focus to each moment of joy oh so clear
Give focus to happiness and strength as they appear
Give focus to the beauty of each day of the year
Cherish and Celebrate Life's Little Triumphs

When My Time is Due

I know God will take me
When My Time is Due
Living life fully
The outcome is true

Enjoying each moment
To the greatest extent
Sharing the beauty
With all beings present

Until then I'll always
Be doing my best
Living life fully
Outpouring with zest

For blessings bestow us
Much kindness to behold
Gifts of joy surround us
Love and friendship abound

I know God will take me
When My Time is Due
Living life fully
The outcome is true

Remarkable Legacy Left Behind

Spirit chose to leave this world
Sadness and difficulty for the rest
Celebration of a wonderful life
Remarkable Legacy Left Behind

Special being greatly loved by all
Touches each heart gently yet profound
Thoughts are changed and life enhanced
Each perspective vision is fully around

Like a diamond crystal clear and bright
Gifts aplenty multifaceted delight
Each one receives to fill their needs
Understanding grows and joy exceeds

As appreciation fills our hearts and minds
Our thoughts and feelings rise up sublime
Gratitude for precious time we've shared
Loving memories nothing can compare

Spirit chose to leave this world
Sadness and difficulty for the rest
Celebration of a wonderful life
Remarkable Legacy Left Behind

Happy Birthday Dear Friend

Happy Birthday Dear Friend
First year since you're gone
Seems like just yesterday
And yet so long ago

Remember your smiling face
Sitting calmly in your special place
Joy you shared with many others
Grateful for your role as friend, wife and mother

Celebration does not seem in order
A few close loved ones all around
A quiet time filled with sweet memories
Thoughts of past fun occasions abound

With loving feelings think of you
Know our relationship is always true
Will miss those moments forever more
An extraordinary person I'll always adore

Happy Birthday Dear Friend
First year since you're gone
Seems like just yesterday
And yet so long ago

Loss of a Soulmate

Loss of a Soulmate
Some time has passed
A need for addiction
Just couldn't let him go

Now that he's really gone
Transitioned from this place
It's difficult for me
To not see him face to face

Partners for life our sacred vows
Shared so much for countless years
Problems began to surface and show
Brought out sorrow and lots of tears

It's time for me to finally release
Know in my heart you're at peace
Give all my love and deepest devotion
To family and friends who are my dearest

Loss of a Soulmate
Some time has passed
A need for addiction
Now I can let him go

A Mother's Love

No matter what we've said and done
No matter how hard things have become
Our hearts are always intertwined
My love for you will never die

So when you feel a sadness beyond control
And a sense that sorry has not been told
Know with kindness in your heart
That I forgave you from the start

For a Mother's Love is boundless and true
And no regrets or words of sorrow are due
The most important thing to me
Is for you, my child to be happy and free

Forgive yourself for all that has happened
For on my part and in my heart I always knew
Your beauty, your caring and your love was real
My bond of deepest love for you is now and forever eternal

No matter what we've said and done
No matter how hard things have become
Our hearts are always intertwined
My love for you will never die

Father's Love Not Forgotten

Father's Love Not Forgotten
Between a man and his son
No matter what happens
Bond so strong lasts forever

Unspoken words of no concern
Watch as boy grows and he learns
Teen years can be a real challenge
Be the role model and observe

See the child become a man
Meet his wife a union at hand
Son becomes a better person
Meaningful relationships expand

Once the son becomes a father
And his sons begin to play
Value of all his family
Clear and glorious every day

Father's Love Not Forgotten
Between a man and his son
No matter what happens
Bond so strong lasts forever

What Would I Tell My Daughter Dear

What Would I Tell My Daughter Dear
What would she truly need to hear
If we knew the final finale could be near
What would I share and make crystal clear

Focus on love and relationships
Cherish the special ones in your life
Notice small things that give you joy
Communicate caring in all you do

Be forgiving to all around
Refrain from assumptions
They could be unfound
Excuse failings both theirs and yours

Enjoy everything and have loads of fun
Play and frolic and dance and run
Laugh with delight and so much pleasure
Share the wonder every moment a beautiful treasure

What Would I Tell My Daughter Dear
What would she truly need to hear
If we knew the final finale could be near
What would I share and make crystal clear

We Said Goodbye a Thousand Times

Don't be sad about my parting
Don't feel like you never said goodbye
For you and I both know deep in our hearts
That We Said Goodbye a Thousand Times
And shared so much love and joy every day

Be happy that I am now at peace
Be joyful that I have lived a wonderful life
Be happy that we have shared so much together

And remember I am always with you in a thought and a sigh
Every day when you see the beauty in nature think of me
Every day when you see the colorful flowers think of me
Every day when you see a frisky animal prancing around think of me
Every day when you look into the eyes of someone you love think of me

And know beyond a doubt that I am with you in everything you do
And know beyond a doubt that I am with you in everything you say
And know beyond a doubt that I am with you
in every quiet moment of your life

Don't be sad about my parting
Don't feel like you never said goodbye
For you and I both know deep in our hearts
That We Said Goodbye a Thousand Times
And shared so much love and joy every day

Personally Inspired Poetry

If you have enjoyed the poems in *Bring Poetry to Life*, you may be interested in receiving a personally inspired poem created just for you.

Carol Calkins is now offering personally inspired poetry through a co-creative process, utilizing her intuition and the individual's personal essence; she captures the true spirit of the person, special event, or significant moments in your life.

The poems are created to provide a personal connection to the words, images, and emotions felt by the individual. These personally inspired messages will soothe and heal your heart, mind, and spirit.

To inquire about co-creating your personally inspired poem, please email Carol at carol@carolcalkins.com

About the Author

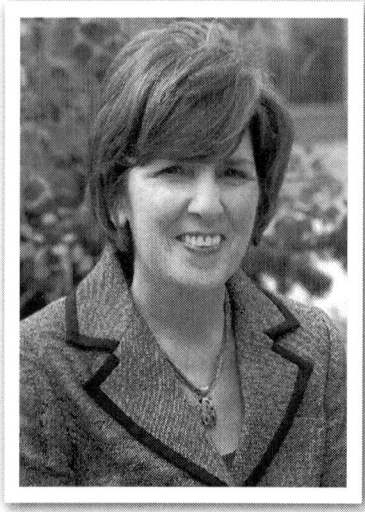

Carol Calkins, PhD has devoted over 30 years toward her management career in the healthcare and higher education professions. Alongside her wonderful husband Mike she lives in beautiful Colorado. Always a family committed to helping others, her daughter and son-in-law Katrina and Ray Dorow are currently living in Johannesburg, South Africa. It was with sheer elation Carol received the news that they are expecting their first child in January 2011. Her first grandchild!

This is just a glimpse of what shapes some of life's most powerful and poignant moments that Carol captures in a few words to mold into a story and create emotion. The title of this book, *Bring Poetry to Life*, represents Carol's enlightening discovery that poetry exists all around us in a look, a smile, a tear and a thought. She began creating personal customized poems for those around her. Carol finally found that her gift to the world is poetry.

Bring Poetry to Life

Special gift was given me
Uncertain from where it came
Presence exists everywhere
Bring Poetry to Life its name

Hear it in people's words
Passing by or dear friends
May be a phrase or in a tone
More than merely facade alone

See it in moments of anxious fear
Or their sadness and their tears
Find in joyful laughter and glee
Brings forth great meaning to me

Sense it as energy surrounds
Creates understanding all around
Vibrations bring great insight too
Immense value for the world and you

Special gift was given me
Uncertain from where it came
Presence exists everywhere
Bring Poetry to Life its name

6438546R0

Made in the USA
Charleston, SC
25 October 2010